THE BEST P COOKBOOK FOR BEGINNERS 2 IN 1

100 DELICIOUS AND HEALTHY RECIPES

TERRY PARSONS, KENNARD GRANT

Table of Contents

INTRODUCTION 11

POTATO SALAD RECIPES 13

   1. Potato salad with herring and apple 13

   2. Frankfurter sausages on potato salad 15

   3. Colorful potato salad.................................17

   4. Chicken and Potato Salad 19

   5. Bavarian potato salad 21

   6. Potato and Egg Salad.................................23

   7. Potato and ham salad.................................25

   8. Potato and radish salad..............................27

   9. Green potato salad....................................29

   10. Potato salad with cucumber 31

POTATO PAN RECIPES 33

   11. Fried potato and asparagus pan...................33

   12. Fish and potato pan with bacon...................35

   13. Fried potatoes with garlic.........................37

   14. Zucchini Potato Tortilla 39

   15. Green potato pan 41

   16. Lamb and potato ragout 43

POTATO COOKED RECIPES 45

   17. Potato casserole with bacon from the steamer
  45

18. pumpkin cream soup 47

19. Pork loin on pumpkin herb 49

20. Potato soup with fresh herbs from the steamer 51

21. Herbal Potato Soup.................................53

22. Meat dumplings......................................55

23. Potato dumplings from the steamer.................57

24. Potato salad with pumpkin seed oil 59

25. Baby food: Pumpkin, potato and lamb porridge 61

26. Potato soup...63

27. Sweet potato rolls 65

28. Wild garlic foam soup 67

29. Minced beef patties from the steamer............69

30. Green asparagus and lemon soup from the steamer 71

31. Potato soup with sausages.......................73

32. pumpkin cream soup...............................75

33. Potato soup with tofu skewers 77

34. Alkaline potato soup...............................79

35. Cabbage potato soup 81

POTATO FRUIT RECIPES...........................83

36. Creamy potato and apple salad 83

37. Apple and celery soup with a celery chip 85

38. Potato choux pastry rings.......................87

39. Pear and potatoes with green beans 89

40. Mango chilli sweet potato soup...................91

41. Herring salad with orange 93

42. Herring salad with grapes........................95

43. Herring salad with avocado 97

44. Roast leg of goose with red cabbage and plum dumplings 99

45. South Tyrolean apricot dumplings 101

46.Cream of blood orange and carrot soup...........103

47. Colorful potato mayonnaise salad...............105

48. Potato noodles 107

49. Apple pie with potato topping 109

50. Potatoes with applesauce.........................112

CONCLUSION 114

INTRODUCTION 117

POTATOES RECIPES MAIN DISH................ 120

1. Potatoes with curd cheese.........................120

2. Baked potatoes 122

3. Szeged gulyas with potatoes 124

4. Braised chicken with potatoes 126

5. Black cumin potatoes with mint raita 128

6. Potato in the beauty bath 130

7. Potato balm for the soul............................132

8. Baked potato eggs...134

9. potato pan 136

10. Cremefine potato and pear gratin....................138

POTATOES RECIPES SEA FOOD AND FISH 140

11. Baked potatoes with herring salad 140

12. Matjes fillets with new potatoes and brunch.143

13. Herbal fish with potato zucchini vegetables..145

14. Salmon fillet with asparagus and vegetables..147

15. Spring salmon from the steamer.....................149

16. Salmon in a bed of vegetables.........................151

17. Herring salad with pomegranate.....................153

18. Char with wild garlic coconut puree.................155

19.Gröstl from the smoked catfish.......................157

20. Carp in black beer batter with green potato
salad...159

POTATOES RECIPES BEEF AND SOUP........... 161

21.Minced meat with mashed potatoes..................161

22. Meat dumplings...163

23. Spinach with boiled beef and roasted potatoes
....165

24. Roast onion with mashed potatoes..................167

25. Liver and potato dumplings with lettuce 169

26. Root vegetable soup with potatoes..................171

27. Potato and mushroom soup 173

28. Potato soup 175

29. Potato soup with chanterelles 177

30. Cabbage potato soup 179

31. Potato soup with sausages 181

32. pumpkin cream soup 183

33. Potato soup with tofu skewers 185

34. Alkaline potato soup 187

35. Broad bean stew 189

POTATOES RECIPES SNACKS 191

36. Sweet potato rolls 191

37. Potato spirals on a skewer 193

38. Potato spread 195

39. Skordalia (potato and garlic paste) 197

40. Alkaline wild garlic wedges 199

41. Herring salad with celery 201

42. Light onion spread with apple and bacon 203

43. Herring salad with pear and nuts 205

44. Herring salad with melon 207

45. Potato buns 209

46. Potato Vegetable Strudel 211

47. Herring salad with orange 213

48. Herring salad with grapes 215

49. Herring salad with avocado 217

7

50. fried potatoes 219

51. Braised chicken with potatoes 221

52. Liver and potato dumplings with lettuce 223

CONCLUSION **225**

THE ULTIMATE POTATO DIET COOKBOOK

50 SIMPLE AND TASTY POTATO RECIPES TO RESET YOUR METABOLISM

TERRY PARSONS

INTRODUCTION

The potato diet is one of the carbohydrate-rich mono-diets, i.e. a diet that consists almost or exclusively of a certain food. There are different variations of the potato diet. They all have in common the main consumption of potatoes, often in combination with eggs or quark. With some diet variants, low-fat vegetables, salad or some fruit are also allowed. In addition to the high intake of potatoes, the low-fat preparation of the dishes is the most important characteristic of the potato diet.

This is how the potato diet works

One kilogram of low-fat potatoes and - depending on the variant - 100 grams of quark or three eggs end up on the plate every day with the potato diet. The combination of potatoes with quark or egg results in a high biological value. This means that the body can absorb and use the protein it contains particularly well. This in turn ensures long-lasting satiety. At the same time, the potassium contained in the potato removes more water from the body. So you lose the first pounds quickly - a point win for the potato.

Potato diet: why the potato is healthy

Potatoes look inconspicuous, but the tuber contains many healthy ingredients: It is rich in vitamins C and B, contains folic acid, copper, phosphate and sulfur. Due to the high potassium content, potatoes have a dehydrating effect.

The long-chain carbohydrates in potatoes are slowly broken down during the digestion process - therefore the tubers keep you full for a long time and prevent cravings. In addition, potatoes hardly contain any fat, but they contain high-quality protein, which can be converted relatively easily into the body's protein.

The best (because they have the lowest calories) ways to prepare potatoes as diet food are potatoes cooked in the oven, jacket potatoes, and potatoes cooled down again. Toppings with low-fat quark or crème légère as well as fresh garden herbs or small chopped raw vegetables such as cucumber, celery or carrots provide variety and provide additional vitamins and minerals.

If you don't want to do without the crispy variations, sprinkle pre-cooked potato wedges with a few drops of olive oil and then grill them in the oven until golden brown. French fries and fried potatoes have been deleted without replacement, as

1. Potato salad with herring and apple

ingredients

- 700 g waxy potatoes
- salt
- 2 apples z. b. boskop
- 2 tbsp lemon juice
- 150 g mustard pickle jar
- 1 bunch chives
- 400 g herring fillet pickled in oil
- 5 tbsp mayonnaise
- 2 tbsp natural yoghurt
- 2 tbsp sour cream
- pepper from the mill
- sugar

Preparation steps

1. Wash the potatoes and cook in salted boiling water for about 25 minutes. Drain, allow to evaporate and peel. Let cool down completely.
2. Wash the apples, quarter them, remove the core, cut into small pieces and mix with 1 tablespoon of lemon juice. Drain the mustard pickles well and cut into bite-sized pieces.
3. Wash the chives, shake dry and cut into rolls. Drain the fish fillets well and also cut into small pieces.
4. Mix the mayonnaise with the yoghurt, sour cream, and lemon juice and season with salt, pepper, and a pinch of sugar. Cut the potatoes into bite-sized pieces and mix with the fish, apples, cucumber and the salad dressing. Arrange in plates and serve sprinkled with chives.

2. Frankfurter sausages on potato salad

ingredients

- 1 kg waxy potatoes
- 1 large onion
- ½ fret radish
- 2 tbsp chives rolls
- 4 tbsp white wine vinegar
- 6 tbsp meatsoup
- 1 tsp mustard
- salt
- freshly ground pepper
- 6 tbsp sunflower oil
- 4 pairs wiener sausages
- chives roll for garnish

Preparation steps

1. Wash the potatoes, cook in the skin for approx. 30 minutes, peel them, let them cool down a little and cut into slices. Peel onions and cut them into fine pieces. Clean and wash the radishes and cut into 3 mm wide sticks.
2. For the dressing, mix vinegar with the broth. Stir in mustard, salt and pepper. Stir in the oil. Carefully mix the onions, radishes and the potato slices with the sauce and let the salad steep for about 15 minutes, garnish with chives.
3. Warm the sausages in hot water (do not boil) and serve.

3. Colorful potato salad

ingredients

- 600 g waxy potatoes
- 2 red onions
- 3 tbsp apple cider vinegar
- iodized salt with fluoride
- pepper
- ½ tsp dried marjoram
- 150 ml vegetable broth
- 1 tbsp mustard
- 1 tbsp apple syrup
- 2 tbsp olive oil
- 1 cucumber
- 2 carrots
- 1 red apple
- 10 g parsley (0.5 bunch)

Preparation steps

1. Cook the potatoes in boiling water for 20–30 minutes. Then drain, quench, peel while hot and let cool. While the potatoes are boiling, peel and finely dice the onions. Bring the onion cubes to the boil with vinegar, salt, pepper, marjoram and broth. Whisk in the mustard, syrup and oil.

2. Cut the potatoes into slices. Pour the dressing over the potatoes and let it steep for 30 minutes, stirring gently more often.

3. In the meantime, clean and wash the cucumber, cut in half lengthways, scrape out the seeds with a teaspoon and cut the cucumber into fine slices. Clean, wash, peel and roughly grate the carrots. Clean, wash, halve and core the apple and cut into small pieces.

4. Mix the cucumber, carrots and apple with the potatoes, season with salt and pepper and let the salad stand for another 10 minutes.

5. Wash the parsley, shake dry, pluck the leaves off, chop finely and mix with the potato salad.

4. Chicken and Potato Salad

ingredients

- 20 g sultanas
- 350 g chicken breast fillet (2 chicken breast fillets)
- salt
- pepper
- 1 tbsp olive oil
- 25 g pine nuts
- 30 g black olives marinated dry, without stone
- 250 g waxy potatoes
- 3 tbsp light pesto
- 3 stems basil
- 75 g mild sheep cheese

Preparation steps

1. Soak the sultanas in a small bowl covered with warm water for 10 minutes.
2. Wash the chicken breasts, pat dry and season with salt and pepper.
3. Heat the oil in a pan and fry the meat for 3 minutes on each side. Add water until the bottom of the pan is covered and cook the meat covered for another 4 minutes over medium heat. If necessary, add a little water.
4. Let the chicken cool and cut the meat into 1 cm cubes.
5. Lightly toast the pine nuts in a pan without fat. Roughly chop the olives.
6. Squeeze the sultanas, roughly chop and mix with the prepared ingredients in a bowl.
7. Wash, peel and cut the potatoes into 1.5 cm cubes, add to boiling salted water and cook for 9 minutes.
8. Remove 2 tablespoons of potato water and mix with the pesto.
9. Drain the potatoes, drain well and mix with the other ingredients with the pesto, season with salt and pepper and leave to steep for 10 minutes.
10. Wash the basil, shake dry, pluck the leaves and roughly chop. Crumble the sheep's cheese. Sprinkle both over the salad just before serving.

5. Bavarian potato salad

ingredients

- 1 kg waxy potatoes
- 1 onion
- 50 g pickled cucumber (1 pickled cucumber)
- 300 ml broth (preferably meat broth)
- 4 tbsp white wine vinegar
- 2 tsp medium hot mustard
- salt
- pepper
- 4 tbsp rapeseed oil
- 8 70 g turkey wiener (5% fat)
- 1 bunch chives
- 80 g lamb's lettuce

Preparation steps

1. Wash the potatoes and cook them with the skin in boiling water for 20-30 minutes, depending on their size, not too soft.

2. In the meantime, peel and dice the onion. Pat the gherkin dry and dice it too.
3. Drain the potatoes, rinse thoroughly under running cold water and allow to cool for about 5 minutes. Then peel, cut into thin slices and place in a large bowl.
4. Bring the broth and onion cubes to the boil in a small saucepan. Take off the stove. Beat 3 tablespoons of vinegar, mustard, salt, pepper and oil with a whisk.
5. Pour the mixture over the potatoes while it is still hot. Add the pickled cucumber, mix everything carefully and let it steep for at least 30 minutes.
6. Just before serving, heat the water in a large saucepan, but do not let it boil. Let the sausages get hot for about 10 minutes over a low heat.
7. In the meantime, wash the chives, shake dry and cut into rolls. Clean and wash lamb's lettuce, spin dry and pluck a little smaller if you like.
8. Fold the lamb's lettuce and chives into the potato salad. Season again with salt, pepper and the rest of the vinegar. Take the sausages out of the pot and serve with the potato salad.

6. Potato and Egg Salad

ingredients

- 700 g waxy potatoes
- salt
- 4 eggs
- 2 poles celery
- 1 onion
- 2 apples z. b. boskop
- 2 tbsp lemon juice
- 300 g natural yoghurt
- 200 g mayonnaise
- 1 tbsp dijon mustard
- pepper from the mill

Preparation steps

1. Cook the potatoes in boiling salted water for about 25 minutes. Drain, allow to evaporate and peel while it is still hot. Boil the eggs in

water for 10 minutes, drain, rinse in cold water and peel.

2. Wash and clean the celery, halve lengthways and cut into thin slices. Peel the onion and finely chop. Wash the apples, quarter them, remove the cores and cut into bite-sized pieces. Mix immediately with lemon juice.

3. Mix the yogurt with the mayonnaise and mustard and season with salt and pepper. Cut the potatoes into large cubes, chop the eggs and mix with the potatoes, celery, apples, onions and the salad cream, season again to taste and serve in a dish.

7. Potato and ham salad

ingredients
- 1 kg waxy potatoes
- 4 tbsp olives
- sea-salt
- pepper from the mill
- 2 tbsp lemon juice
- 150 g feta
- 100 g parma ham thinly sliced

for the set
- 2 branches thyme
- 2 untreated lemons

Preparation steps
1. Preheat the oven to 200 ° C fan-assisted air. Wash the potatoes thoroughly, cut in half or quarter and spread on a baking sheet lined with baking paper.

2. Drizzle with the oil, season with salt, pepper, mix and bake in the oven for about 30 minutes until golden brown. From time to time to turn. Take out of the oven and let cool down lukewarm.
3. Drizzle with the lemon juice and season with salt and pepper. Mix loosely with the crumbled feta and ham and garnish with thyme and lemon halves (in glasses if you like).

8. Potato and radish salad

ingredients

- 800 g waxy potatoes
- 1 red onion
- 1 handful arugula
- 1 bunch radish
- $\frac{1}{2}$ fret herbs (dill, parsley or chives)
- 200 ml vegetable broth
- 3 tbsp apple cider vinegar
- 3 tbsp olive oil
- salt
- pepper

Preparation steps

1. Cook the potatoes in boiling water for 20–30 minutes. Then drain, quench, peel while hot and let cool.

2. Meanwhile, peel the red onion and dice it finely. Wash the rocket and shake dry. Clean and wash the radishes and cut into thin slices. Wash herbs, shake dry and chop. Bring the vegetable stock to the boil.
3. Cut the potatoes into slices. In a large bowl, combine with the hot vegetable stock, onions, vinegar, olive oil, salt, and pepper. Then let it steep for at least 30 minutes.
4. Fold the prepared radishes, rocket and herbs into the potato salad before serving and season with salt and pepper.

9. Green potato salad

ingredients

- 300 g waxy potatoes (3 waxy potatoes)
- salt
- 1 red onion
- 2 tbsp apple cider vinegar
- 150 ml classic vegetable broth
- 2 tbsp rapeseed oil
- pepper
- 80 g lamb's lettuce
- 1 bunch chives
- 1 apple
- 70 g salmon ham

Preparation steps

1. Wash the potatoes and cook in boiling water for 20-25 minutes. Then drain, rinse under cold water, peel and let cool.

2. Cut the cooled potatoes into slices, season with salt and place in a bowl. Peel onion and chop finely.
3. Bring the onion cubes with vinegar and broth to the boil in a small saucepan, pour boiling over the potatoes.
4. Add the oil and mix everything. Let it steep for 30 minutes, mixing more often.
5. In the meantime, clean the lamb's lettuce, leaving the roots intact so that the leaves stay together. Wash the lettuce and spin dry thoroughly. Wash the chives, shake dry and cut into fine rolls.
6. Wash, quarter and core the apple and cut into fine wedges.
7. Cut the salmon ham into fine strips.
8. Season the potato salad with salt and pepper. Add the lamb's lettuce, chives rolls, ham strips and apple slices to the salad and mix in.

10. Potato salad with cucumber

ingredients

- 800 g waxy potatoes
- salt
- ½ cucumber
- 2 small onions
- 125 ml meatsoup
- 1 tsp hot mustard
- 4 tbsp white wine vinegar
- pepper from the mill
- 1 bunch chives
- 5 tbsp olive oil

Preparation steps

1. Wash the potatoes and cook in salted boiling water for about 25 minutes.
2. In the meantime, wash the cucumber, halve lengthways, cut into thin slices and sprinkle

with salt. Let it steep for about 20 minutes and squeeze it out.

3. Peel the onions, cut into fine cubes, and boil with the stock in a saucepan. Stir in the mustard and vinegar, season with salt, pepper and remove from the stove.

4. Drain the potatoes, allow to evaporate, peel and let cool. Then cut into slices, pour the hot stock over them, mix carefully and let stand for about 20 minutes.

5. Rinse the chives, shake dry and cut into fine rolls. Mix with the cucumber and oil into the salad, season again to taste and serve on a plate.

11. Fried potato and asparagus pan

ingredients

- 800 g small mainly waxy potatoes
- iodized salt with fluoride
- 400 g green asparagus
- 4 shallots
- 15 g clarified butter (1 tbsp)
- 3 stems parsley
- pepper

Preparation steps

1. Wash potatoes and cook in salted water for 15 minutes.

2. In the meantime, wash the asparagus, peel the lower third, cut off the woody ends. Cook the asparagus in boiling salted water for about 8 minutes. Drain, drain, then cut diagonally into pieces.
3. Drain the potatoes, let them evaporate and cut in half lengthways.
4. Peel shallots and cut into wedges.
5. Heat the clarified butter in a high pan. Fry the potatoes in it over a medium heat, turning regularly, until golden brown for 10 minutes.
6. In the meantime, wash the parsley, shake dry and chop.
7. Mix the shallots with the potatoes and fry for 4 minutes. Mix in the asparagus and fry for 2 minutes, turning more often.
8. Season the fried potato and asparagus pan with salt, pepper and parsley.

12. Fish and potato pan with bacon

ingredients

- 500 g waxy potatoes
- salt
- 500 g white fish fillet z. b. cod
- 1 onion
- 120 g smoked pork belly in cubes
- 20 g butter pepper from the mill
- 2 tbsp freshly chopped parsley

Preparation steps

1. Wash the potatoes and cook in salted boiling water for about 20 minutes. Drain, rinse in cold water, peel and allow to cool. Wash the fish, pat dry and cut into bite-sized pieces.
2. Peel the onion and cut into fine cubes. Leave the bacon in a pan, add a little butter and

sweat the onion in it until translucent. Cut the potatoes into slices, add and fry until golden brown, turning occasionally. Add the fish pieces and fry them until golden brown, turning them carefully. Season with salt and pepper and serve sprinkled with freshly chopped parsley.

13. Fried potatoes with garlic

ingredients

- 1 kg waxy potatoes
- 150 ml vegetable broth
- salt
- pepper from the mill
- 2 stems rosemary
- 6 garlic cloves
- 4 tbsp olive oil

Preparation steps

1. Preheat the oven to 180 ° C fan oven.
2. Peel the potatoes and cut in halves or quarters depending on the size. Put in a roasting pan and pour in the broth. Season with salt and pepper and stew in the oven for

about 20 minutes. From time to time to turn. The potatoes should be almost cooked and the liquid should be absorbed. Sprinkle the plucked rosemary and the pressed garlic cloves over it and put the olive oil drizzled back in the oven at 220 ° C and brown for 15-20 minutes. Meanwhile, turn back and forth from time to time.

14. Zucchini Potato Tortilla

ingredients

- 175 g potatoes (2 potatoes)
- 250 g zucchini (1 zucchini)
- 1 clove of garlic
- 2 onions
- 45 g serrano ham (3 slices)
- 2 tbsp olive oil
- salt
- pepper
- 4 eggs

Preparation steps

1. Wash the potatoes, cook with the skin for about 15-20 minutes, then peel and cut into 1 cm cubes. While the potatoes are boiling,

wash and clean the zucchini and cut into 1 cm cubes. Peel and finely dice the garlic and onions.

2. Cut the ham into fine strips.
3. Heat the oil in a non-stick pan and sauté the onions and garlic over a medium heat for 1 minute until translucent. Add the potato and zucchini cubes and stir-fry for 4 minutes until they are golden brown, season with salt and pepper.
4. Whisk eggs in a bowl and season lightly with salt and pepper. Pour into the pan, sprinkle with strips of ham and let stand for 3 minutes over medium heat while stirring gently.
5. Turn the tortilla: It is best to turn it out onto a plate and slide it back into the pan. Let stand for another 4 minutes. Serve the tortilla cut into pieces.

15. Green potato pan

ingredients

- 500 g new potatoes
- 1 green pepper
- 3 fresh cloves of garlic
- 1 bunch spring onions
- 75 g green olives (with stone)
- 3 stems basil
- 2 tbsp olive oil
- salt
- pepper
- 50 g sheep cheese
- 1 tsp unpeeled sesame seeds

Preparation steps

1. Scrub the potatoes and cook in boiling water for 20-25 minutes, drain and leave to cool. While the potatoes are boiling, quarter, core and wash the pepper and place on a baking sheet with the skin side up.
2. Roast under the hot grill until the skin turns black and bubbles, pour into a bowl, cover with a plate and let rest for 10 minutes.
3. Peel off the skin and cut the pod into fine strips.
4. Peel the garlic and cut into fine slices.
5. Clean and wash the spring onions and cut into thin slices at a slight angle.
6. Cut the olives into slices from the stone and then into fine sticks.
7. Wash the basil, shake dry, pluck the leaves and chop finely.
8. Halve the potatoes.
9. Heat the oil in a pan and fry the potatoes on the cut surface until golden brown.
10. Add the garlic and paprika and stir-fry for another 2 minutes. Season with salt and pepper.
11. Add the spring onions, olives and basil and heat briefly.
12. Crumble the cheese. Sprinkle the sesame seeds over the potatoes just before serving. Serve the potato pan.

16. Lamb and potato ragout

ingredients

- 500 g lamb (shoulder or leg)
- 500 g potatoes
- 300 g tomatoes
- 4 tbsp olive oil
- 2 tbsp parsley (chopped)
- 1 rosemary sprigs (roughly chopped)
- 1 teaspoon oregano
- 1 onion
- 1 clove of garlic
- Sea salt (from the mill)
- Pepper (from the mill)
- 50 g pecorino (freshly grated)

preparation

1. Divide the lamb into medium-sized pieces. Cut the potatoes into large cubes, the onion into rings and the garlic clove into thin slices. Put the lamb with the potatoes in an ovenproof dish.

2. Scald the tomatoes briefly, peel and cut into small pieces. Mix with olive oil, chopped parsley, rosemary, oregano, onions and garlic. Season with salt and pepper and mix into the meat. Sprinkle everything with freshly grated pecorino cheese and cover the pan with aluminum foil. Cook in the preheated oven at 170 ° C for about 2 hours.

17. Potato casserole with bacon from the steamer

ingredients

- 100 g breakfast bacon
- 1 pc onion
- 2 clove (s) of garlic
- 500 g potatoes
- 1 pc. Paprika (red)
- 1 pc. Paprika (green)
- 1 rosemary sprigs
- 6 pcs. Eggs
- salt
- pepper
- Butter (for greasing)

preparation

1. For the potato casserole, cut the bacon into strips. Peel the onion, cut in half and also cut into strips. Peel the garlic and cut into fine slices. Fry the bacon in a non-stick pan with the onions until crispy and at the end briefly add the garlic. Set the pan aside.

2. Peel the potatoes, cut into $\frac{1}{2}$ cm thick slices, place in the greased, unperforated cooking container with the bacon onions including the frying fat and pre-cook (at 100 ° C for 5 minutes).

3. In the meantime, clean and core the peppers and cut into thin strips.

4. Pluck rosemary needles and chop finely, whisk with eggs, salt and pepper and add to the potato mixture with the paprika strips. Close the cooking container with a lid or aluminum foil. Let the casserole set (at 100 ° C for 25 minutes).

5. Serve the potato casserole hot or cold cut into pieces.

18. pumpkin cream soup

ingredients

- 600 g pumpkin
- 2 potatoes
- 1 clove (s) of garlic (crushed)
- 1/2 onion
- 1 liter of water
- Soup cubes
- salt
- pepper
- ginger
- 125 ml whipped cream
- 1 tbsp crème fraîche
- Pumpkin seeds (and pumpkin seed oil for garnish)

preparation

1. Peel the pumpkin, remove the core and cut the pumpkin flesh into cubes.
2. Peel the potato and also cut it into cubes. Peel and finely chop the onion. Add the pressed garlic.
3. Put everything in a solid container and fill up with 1 liter of water.
4. Season with seasoning, salt, pepper, ginger or ginger powder and cook.
5. Temperature setting: 120 ° C Cooking time: 10 minutes
6. After the cooking time, puree the soup, season again if necessary, add whipped cream and crème fraîche.
7. To garnish, add a few pumpkin seeds and a few drops of pumpkin seed oil to the soup.

19. Pork loin on pumpkin herb

ingredients

- 300 g cabbage (cut into cubes)
- 100 g pumpkin (diced)
- thyme
- 1/2 l beef soup
- 1 pc potatoes (raw)
- Horseradish
- salt
- 1 dash of vinegar
- 1 tbsp sour cream
- 1 pc. Pork fillet
- salt
- mustard

preparation

1. Cook the cabbage and pumpkin in the steamer for approx. 5 - 10 minutes at 100 ° C. For the sauce, cut the potatoes into small pieces, cook them in the beef soup until soft and mix well with horseradish and sour cream. Season with salt and vinegar. Season the pork fillet with salt and mustard and fry on both sides. Cook in the oven at 160 ° for about 15 minutes. Let rest for at least 10 minutes before slicing. Arrange the cabbage and pumpkin on the plates, arrange the fillet pieces on top, sprinkle with herbs and serve with keratin sauce.

20. Potato soup with fresh herbs from the steamer

ingredients

- 180 g leeks
- 250 g potatoes (floury)
- 500 ml vegetable stock
- salt
- pepper
- 100 g of cream
- 2 tbsp herbs (parsley, chives, basil)

preparation

1. First clean the leek and cut into rings. Peel and roughly dice the potatoes.
2. Put both with the vegetable soup in a solid cooking container and cook (at 100 ° C for 16 minutes or 120 ° C for 8 minutes).

3. Puree the soup and season with salt and pepper. Stir in the cream and heat (at 95 ° C for 2 minutes).
4. Chop the herbs, pour over the potato soup and serve.

21. Herbal Potato Soup

ingredients

- 1 bunch of herbs (large)
- 5-6 pcs. Potatoes
- 30 g butter
- 1 onion (peeled)
- 1 l chicken soup (or vegetable soup)
- salt
- pepper
- 6 tbsp chives (cut)
- Creme double (or crème fraîche)

preparation

1. For the herb potato soup, cut the potatoes and onions into small pieces and place in a solid cooking container. Pour in the vegetable

soup and cook the soup at 100 ° C for about 20 minutes.

2. Cut the herbs into small pieces, add them and cook for another 5 minutes at 100 ° C.
3. Mix the soup with the crème fraîche, season to taste again and puree until frothy with the blender.
4. To serve, garnish the herb and potato soup with chives.

22. Meat dumplings

ingredients

For the dough:

- 500 g potatoes
- 10 g butter
- 30 g wheat semolina
- 120 g flour (handy)
- 1 pc egg
- salt
- nutmeg

For the fullness:

- 1 tbsp sunflower oil
- 100 g onions
- 200 g minced meat (mixed)
- 1 tbsp QimiQ
- salt

- Mustard, pepper
- Marjoram, garlic

preparation

1. Prepare the potato dough: peel, quarter and steam the potatoes. Press the potatoes on a floured pastry board, sprinkle the butter in flakes on top and briefly knead together with the remaining ingredients to form a dough.
2. Prepare the filling: finely chop the onions, roast them in oil, add the minced meat, roast briefly, thicken with QimiQ and season.
3. Deliver water.
4. Shape the dough into a roll, cut into slices, spread the filling on top, form the dumplings and close tightly.
5. Let the dumplings soak in salted water for about 10-15 minutes.
6. Take out the meat dumplings with a sieve scoop and serve.

23. Potato dumplings from the steamer

ingredients

- 1 kg of potatoes
- 1-2 pc eggs
- salt
- nutmeg
- 50 g flour
- 50 g potato starch
- Butter (for greasing)

preparation

1. For the potato dumplings, wash the potatoes and cook in a perforated cooking tray (at 100 ° C for 28-34 minutes).

2. Peel the potatoes while they are still hot and press them straight through the potato press.
3. Add the eggs to the potato batter and season with salt and nutmeg. Stir in the flour and potato starch.
4. Shape the dough into a roll and divide into 12-14 pieces. Shape the pieces into dumplings and cook in the greased, perforated cooking tray (at 100 ° C for 15-18 minutes).

24. Potato salad with pumpkin seed oil

ingredients

- 600 g potatoes (Sieglinde or Kipfler, cooked and peeled)
- 60 g onions (finely chopped)
- 1/4 l soup (fat)
- 3 tbsp apple cider vinegar
- 6 tbsp pumpkin seed oil
- salt
- Pepper (black)
- Some tarragon mustard (to taste)

preparation

1. For the potato salad, peel potatoes cooked with pumpkin seed oil while still hot and cut into fine slices.

2. Pour warm soup on immediately, add pumpkin seed oil, onions, vinegar, salt and pepper.
3. Stir the potato salad with pumpkin seed oil vigorously until it is creamy. Add mustard or sugar, depending on your taste.

25. Baby food: Pumpkin, potato and lamb porridge

ingredients

- 60 g pumpkin (e.g. Hokkaido, nutmeg)
- 1 piece of potato
- 20 g of lamb
- Rapeseed oil (a few drops)

preparation

1. Homemade baby food - first complementary food
2. For the pumpkin, potato and lamb porridge, parry the lamb (remove fat and tendons).
3. Peel the pumpkin and potato and cut into cubes.
4. Cook all ingredients in a little water over low heat until soft and puree with the blender.

5. Finally, stir in a few drops of rapeseed oil to the pumpkin, potato and lamb porridge.

26. Potato soup

ingredients

- 500 g potatoes
- 3 carrots
- 500 ml of vegetable soup
- 250 ml whipped cream
- salt
- pepper
- Bay leaf
- marjoram
- Mushrooms for men (can also be dried mushrooms)
- 1/2 onion
- 1 clove (s) of garlic

preparation

1. Cut the potatoes into small pieces. Put the potato pieces with the soup, spices and

mushrooms in an unperforated bowl and steam for about 30 minutes at 100 ° C.

2. In the meantime, wash the carrots and cut them into small pieces.
3. In the remaining 7 minutes of the potato cooking time, also place the carrots in the steamer.
4. Remove the bay leaf and finely puree the potato soup with the blender.
5. If desired, add the whipped cream and season again to taste.

27. Sweet potato rolls

ingredients

- 250 g potatoes (floury)
- 250 g wheat flour (smooth)
- 250 g whole wheat flour
- 1 package dry yeast
- 80 g of sugar
- 1 pc egg
- 80 g yogurt (low fat)
- 1/8 l skimmed milk (lukewarm, or water)

preparation

1. Steam the potatoes in their skins for about 20 minutes. Peel while hot and press through a potato press. Let cool down slightly.
2. Mix in the flour, yeast, sugar, egg and yoghurt. Pour in liquid. At the beginning only about 100ml and the rest only when needed.

Knead the dough vigorously with the food processor for about 5 minutes.

3. If necessary, add a little more liquid so that the dough has a smooth consistency. Cover and let the dough rise in a warm place for approx. 45 - 30 minutes.

4. Then form 15 rolls and place on a perforated, greased (or lined with parchment paper) cooking insert.

28. Wild garlic foam soup

ingredients

- 200 g wild garlic (cut)
- 1-2 potatoes (floury)
- 1 pc onion (small)
- some leek
- 750 ml of vegetable soup
- 200 ml skimmed milk (or soy milk)
- 1 tbsp crème fraîche
- salt
- pepper
- nutmeg

preparation

1. For the wild garlic foam soup, peel the potatoes and cut into small cubes. Cut the

onion and leek and add to the potatoes. Put all the ingredients in an unperforated bowl, add the vegetable soup and steam at 100 ° C for 12-15 minutes.

2. Put the wild garlic (save a few leaves for decoration) in a perforated cooking bowl and blanch for 1 - 2 minutes at 100 ° C and mix with the soup two minutes before the end of the cooking time, as does the milk.

3. At the end of the cooking time, season the soup with salt, pepper and nutmeg, refine with creme fraiche and puree in a blender.

4. Garnish the wild garlic soup with finely chopped wild garlic.

29. Minced beef patties from the steamer

ingredients

- 500 g beef minced meat
- 2 eggs
- 1 onion (small)
- 2 cloves of garlic
- 1 bunch of herbs (fresh, e.g. parsley, thyme, marjoram, etc.)
- 50 g breadcrumbs
- salt
- pepper
- 600 g potatoes
- 100 ml water (hot)
- 2 tbsp Dijon mustard
- Herbs (fresh, two handfuls)

preparation

1. For the steamed minced beef patties, peel the onion and garlic and chop very finely. Wash and finely chop herbs.
2. Mix the minced meat with the eggs, onions, garlic, herbs and breadcrumbs, knead well and season with salt and pepper. Shape minced patties or balls.
3. Peel the potatoes and cut into cubes. Mix the mustard with hot water, add the herbs and season with salt.
4. Put the potato cubes in a solid container and mix with the mustard marinade. Place the minced patties on the potatoes and steam everything at 100 ° for 25 minutes.
5. Stir the steamed minced beef patties well again before serving.

30. Green asparagus and lemon soup from the steamer

ingredients

- 350 g green asparagus
- 200 g potatoes (floury)
- 1 1/2 tbsp soup cubes
- 1/2 lemon (juice and zest)
- 650 ml of water
- 125 ml cream
- Worcestershire Sauce
- salt
- pepper
- Chive flowers (to decorate)

preparation

1. For the asparagus-lemon soup, wash the asparagus, cut into pieces and put the tips aside.

2. Peel and chop the potatoes.
3. Put the asparagus pieces, potatoes, water, soup seasoning, lemon juice and zest in a non-perforated steamer and steam at 100 ° C for 12 minutes. Steam the asparagus tips in a perforated insert for the last 3 minutes.
4. Puree the soup, mix in the cream and season with Worcesthire sauce, salt and pepper.
5. Place the asparagus tips in the finished asparagus-lemon soup and serve with chive flowers.

31. Potato soup with sausages

ingredients

- 1 pack of Tk soup green
- 800 g potatoes
- 1 onion
- 30 g butter
- 750 ml beef soup ((instant))
- 125 ml whipped cream
- salt
- pepper
- Paprika (noble sweet)
- 4 frankfurters
- 1 bunch of parsley

preparation

1. Defrost the soup greens. Peel and rinse potatoes, cut into cubes. Peel and chop the

onion, sauté in butter until translucent. Add potatoes and fry briefly. Pour in clear soup, cook everything together for 12-15 minutes.

2. Remove 1/3 of the potatoes, grind the rest in the saucepan. Put the remaining potato pieces with the thawed soup greens and whipped cream in the saucepan again. Soup 6-8 min.

3. Season with peppers, salt and pepper. Sauté Frankfurt sausages in hot water, remove and drain. Cut into small slices. In the potato soup form. Rinse the parsley, shake dry, chop finely and sprinkle over it before serving.

32. pumpkin cream soup

ingredients

- 1 pumpkin (Hokaido)
- 2 onions
- 2 cloves of garlic
- 5 potatoes
- 1 l vegetable soup
- 250 ml sour cream (or 200 ml whipped cream)
- Pumpkin seed oil
- salt

preparation

1. For the pumpkin cream soup, finely chop the onion and garlic. Cut the pumpkin and potato into small pieces.
2. Heat oil in a large saucepan and lightly sweat the onion pieces and garlic. Pour on the soup and bring to the boil. Add the pumpkin and potato pieces and simmer for 20 minutes.
3. Puree the soup after the 20 minutes. Stir in the sour cream or whipped cream well and season with salt.
4. Arrange in a soup plate and decorate the pumpkin cream soup with the pumpkin seed oil.

33. Potato soup with tofu skewers

ingredients

- 750 g potatoes
- 3 pcs. Onions
- 2 tbsp olive oil
- 1 l vegetable soup
- 2 zucchini (small)
- 200 g tofu
- 1 tbsp sesame seeds
- salt
- 250 ml soy (cooking cream)
- 1 tbsp mustard
- marjoram
- pepper

preparation

1. For the potato soup with tofu skewers, peel and chop the potatoes and onions. Heat 1 tbsp oil in a saucepan and sauté the onion briefly.
2. Add the potatoes, deglaze with the soup. Bring to the boil and cook for 15 minutes. Cut the zucchini and tofu into slices and stick them alternately on wooden skewers.
3. Fry the skewers in the hot oil until golden brown while turning. Sprinkle with sesame seeds and season with salt and pepper.
4. Puree the soup, mix the cooking cream and mustard and add to the soup, bring to the boil again. Season with salt and pepper.
5. The potato soup with tofu skewers serve.

34. Alkaline potato soup

ingredients

- 500 ml of water
- 1 vegetable soup cube
- 1 pinch of acerola powder
- 8 potatoes (medium)
- 100 g carrots (finely grated)
- 1 leek (leek, stick)
- 1 kg onion (finely chopped)
- 2 tbsp cream
- 1 tbsp dille (fresh, finely chopped)
- 1 tbsp butter
- sea-salt
- 1 pinch of pepper
- 1 pinch of paprika powder

preparation

1. For the alkaline potato soup, sauté the onion in butter until translucent. Pour water on.
2. Add potatoes and finely chopped vegetables and bring everything to a boil.
3. Simmer on a low level for 15 minutes and then puree. Refine with cream and season with the spices.
4. Sprinkle the finely chopped dill on top.
5. The acerola powder just before Servierenin the Basic Potato Soup add.

35. Cabbage potato soup

ingredients

- 500 g potatoes
- 3 onions
- 750 g white cabbage (sliced)
- 1 liter of soup
- 500 g bacon (lean)
- 3 tbsp caraway seeds
- 1 tbsp flour
- 1 tbsp butter
- 3 tbsp sour cream
- 1 tbsp salt
- pepper

preparation

1. For the cabbage potato soup, sauté grated white cabbage, peeled potatoes and lean bacon cut into cubes in the soup until soft. Season to taste with salt, caraway seeds and pepper.
2. Before serving, sauté the finely chopped onions in a little butter, dust with flour, stir with a little sour cream and stir into the cabbage-potato soup .

36. Creamy potato and apple salad

ingredients

- 500 g potatoes (cooked and peeled)
- 2 apples
- 2 carrots
- 2 stalk (s) spring onions (large)
- 1 bunch of mint (small)
- 2 tbsp raisins
- 2 tbsp almond sticks
- 1 orange
- 250 g yoghurt (natural)
- 1 tbsp curry powder
- 2 cloves of garlic (peeled)
- salt

- pepper
- olive oil

preparation

1. Cut the cooked, peeled potatoes into thin slices. Quarter and core the apples and also cut into very fine slices. Put the apples and potatoes in a large bowl and season with a little salt.
2. Peel the carrots and grate finely. Clean the spring onions and cut diagonally into very fine rings. Add the carrots and spring onions to the bowl.
3. Cut the mint into fine strips and add to the potatoes with the raisins and almond sticks.
4. Peel the orange with a knife, cut out the fillets and collect the juice. Mix this with the yogurt, curry powder, finely chopped garlic, salt, pepper and a little olive oil to a marinade and pour over the salad.
5. Mix everything carefully and let it steep for about 10 minutes.
6. Season the salad with salt and serve garnished with the orange fillets.

37. Apple and celery soup with a celery chip

ingredients

For the soup:

- 500 g celery
- 1 apple
- 1 potatoes
- 100 ml apple juice
- 100 ml whipped cream
- 500 ml vegetable soup (or water)
- 1 tbsp vegetable soup (grainy)
- salt

For the chips:

- 100 g celery
- 250 ml of olive oil

preparation

1. For the apple and celery soup with celery chips, first preheat the steamer or combination steamer to 100 ° C.
2. Peel the celery, apple and potato and cut into large cubes. Place in an unperforated cooking container and steam at 100 ° C for 5 minutes.
3. Now add the apple cubes, apple juice, whipped cream, vegetable stock, granulated vegetable stock, and salt: steam for another 10 minutes. Then finely puree the soup with the hand blender (or in the stand mixer) and season to taste again.
4. For the celery chips, cut the celery into thin slices and fry them in hot fat to make chips, drain briefly on kitchen paper, and then serve the soup.
5. Serve apple and celery soup with a celery chip.

38. Potato choux pastry rings

ingredients

For the mashed potatoes:

- 300 g potatoes
- nutmeg
- 2 tbsp milk
- 1 teaspoon salt
- pepper

For the choux pastry:

- 100 ml of water
- 100 ml milk
- 80 g butter
- 100 g of flour
- 3 eggs (size M)
- salt
- pepper

- 1 egg yolk
- 2 tbsp milk

preparation

1. For the potato choux pastry rings, peel the potatoes, boil them and let them cool.
2. In the meantime, bring the water and milk to the boil. Add the butter and let it melt. When the butter has melted, add the flour all at once and stir vigorously with a wooden spoon.
3. It gets a bit crumbly initially, but after 3-4 minutes a dough ball forms. Place this ball in a bowl and stir in the eggs, one at a time. Stir for another 5 minutes, until everything is nice and creamy. Then add salt and pepper.
4. Mash the cold potatoes (coarse or very fine, depending on your taste). Rub in a little nutmeg and add 2 tablespoons of milk, stir and season with salt and pepper.
5. Preheat the oven to 190 ° C fan oven. Now carefully stir the puree and choux pastry together with the spatula. Place in a piping bag with a large nozzle and squirt small rings about 8 cm in diameter onto a baking sheet lined with baking paper.
6. Mix the egg yolk and 2 tbsp milk and brush the rings with it. Bake on the middle rack for 30 minutes until golden brown.

39. Pear and potatoes with green beans

ingredients

- 2 pears
- 250 g green beans
- 600 g potatoes (new)
- 170 ml of oil
- 1 star anise
- 20 g pine nuts (roasted)
- 40 basil leaves
- 1 bunch of parsley (smooth)
- 30 g of sugar
- 1 clove of garlic
- 250 ml white wine
- 1 saffron thread
- salt
- pepper

preparation

1. For pear and potatoes with green beans, bring wine, sugar, star anise and saffron to the boil. Peel the pears, cut sixths and stone them. Soak in the spice stock for 10 minutes at a medium temperature and then leave to cool.
2. Coarsely chop the herbs. Roughly chop the pine nuts and garlic, puree with 150 ml oil and salt in a tall container with a hand blender. Add herbs and mix thoroughly. Cover and put in a cool place.
3. Wash the green beans, remove the stalks and cook in boiling salted water for 8-10 minutes. Let cool and drain. Brush the potatoes, halve if necessary, and cook (or steam) in boiling salted water for 20 minutes, drain and let steam out.
4. Heat the rest of the oil in a pan. Fry the beans and potatoes in it for 5 minutes, season with salt and pepper. Strain and add the pears.
5. Cover pear and potatoes with green beans with the pesto and serve.

40. Mango chilli sweet potato soup

ingredients

- 2 pears
- 250 g green beans
- 600 g potatoes (new)
- 170 ml of oil
- 1-star anise
- 20 g pine nuts (roasted)
- 40 basil leaves
- 1 bunch of parsley (smooth)
- 30 g of sugar
- 1 clove of garlic
- 250 ml white wine
- 1 saffron thread
- salt
- pepper

preparation

1. For pear and potatoes with green beans, bring wine, sugar, star anise and saffron to the boil. Peel the pears, cut sixths and stone them. Soak in the spice stock for 10 minutes at a medium temperature and then leave to cool.
2. Coarsely chop the herbs. Roughly chop the pine nuts and garlic, puree with 150 ml oil and salt in a tall container with a hand blender. Add herbs and mix thoroughly. Cover and put in a cool place.
3. Wash the green beans, remove the stalks and cook in boiling salted water for 8-10 minutes. Let cool and drain. Brush the potatoes, halve if necessary, and cook (or steam) in boiling salted water for 20 minutes, drain and let steam out.
4. Heat the rest of the oil in a pan. Fry the beans and potatoes in it for 5 minutes, season with salt and pepper. Strain and add the pears.
5. Cover pear and potatoes with green beans with the pesto and serve.

41. Herring salad with orange

ingredients

- 8 pieces of herring fillets
- 200 g potatoes (cooked)
- 2 pieces of orange
- salt
- 1 onion (small, chopped)
- 1 teaspoon sugar
- 3 tbsp vinegar
- 250 g sour cream
- 4 tbsp mayonnaise
- pepper

preparation

1. Debone and dry the herring fillets. Cut the fillets into small cubes.
2. Peel the oranges, remove the white skin and cut out fine pieces of fillet. Peel and dice the boiled potatoes.
3. Whisk the mayonnaise with the sour cream, vinegar, sugar, pepper and salt. Peel and finely chop the onion and stir into the sauce.
4. Fold the herrings, orange pieces and potatoes into the sour cream mixture.
5. Let it steep for about 1 hour and then serve.

42. Herring salad with grapes

ingredients

- 8 pieces of herring fillets
- 200 g potatoes (cooked)
- 300 g of grapes
- 3 tbsp vinegar
- 250 g sour cream
- 4 tbsp mayonnaise
- pepper
- salt
- 1 onion (small, chopped)
- sugar

preparation

1. Debone and dry the herring fillets. Cut the fillets into small cubes.
2. Halve the individual grapes. Peel and dice the boiled potatoes.
3. Whisk the mayonnaise with the sour cream, vinegar, sugar, pepper and salt. Peel and finely chop the onion and stir into the sauce.
4. Fold the herrings, pieces of grapes and potatoes into the sour cream mixture.
5. Let it steep for about 1 hour and then serve.

43. Herring salad with avocado

ingredients

- 8 pieces of herring fillets
- 200 g potatoes (cooked)
- 1 apple
- 4 tbsp mayonnaise
- 250 g sour cream
- pepper
- salt
- 1 onion (small, chopped)
- 1 teaspoon sugar
- 3 tbsp vinegar
- 2 pieces avocado

preparation

1. Debone and dry the herring fillets. Cut the fillets into small cubes.

2. Peel and dice the apple and the boiled potatoes.
3. Peel the avocado and cut the pulp into small pieces.
4. Whisk the mayonnaise with the sour cream, vinegar, sugar, pepper and salt. Peel and finely chop the onion and stir into the sauce.
5. Fold the herrings, apple pieces, avocado pieces and potatoes into the sour cream mixture.
6. Let it steep for about 1 hour and then serve.

44. Roast leg of goose with red cabbage and plum dumplings

ingredients

- 4 goose legs (each 350 g)
- 150 g root vegetables (carrot, onion, leek, celery)
- 3 Mugwort
- 250 ml poultry stock
- 520 g potato dumpling mixture (finished product)
- 8 prunes
- 4 teaspoons of powder
- 400 g red cabbage (glass)
- 1 tbsp cranberries
- 100 ml currant juice
- 1 apple
- 1 tbsp olive oil

- salt
- pepper

preparation

1. Combine the goose legs in an ovenproof frying pan, pierce both sides with wooden sticks so that the fat runs out, season lightly with salt. Remove the legs, pour off the fat. Briefly touch the root vegetables in the frying pan *, add mugwort, place the legs on top, pour the brown poultry stock and cook in the stove at around 180 ° C for 60 minutes.
2. Form dumplings from the potato mixture, press in an opening, fill the dried plums with Powidl, press into the opening, coat well and soak in light, bubbly salted water until they float on top. Heat the red cabbage, refine with cranberries and currant juice.
3. Clean the apple, cut out the house, cut into wedges and briefly toast in hot goose fat on both sides. Pour off the sauce, pour it onto a flat plate as a mirror, place the leg on top, line up apple wedges, serve red cabbage and dumplings next to it, garnish with a sprig of mugwort.

45. South Tyrolean apricot dumplings

ingredients

- 1000 g potatoes
- 80 g butter
- 50 g semolina
- 1 egg
- 2 yolks
- 250 g of flour
- 1500 g apricots or plums
- Sugar (cubes)
- salt
- To serve:
- 180 g butter
- 150 g breadcrumbs
- Cinnamon (powder)

preparation

1. Cook the potatoes in the skin until soft and remove them from the skin while still hot.
2. Press through the potato press and let cool a little. Then mix the potato mixture with the butter, semolina, salt, egg and yolks.
3. Sift the flour into the amount and prepare the whole thing to a smooth dough (maybe add a little flour). Rest a few minutes.
4. Flour the surface, roll out the dough on it half a centimeter thick and cut out 7x7cm squares. Replace the core of the apricots with a sugar lump and cover with the dough squares.
5. Make the dumplings in boiling salted water and at a very low temperature for about 10 minutes. Melt the butter and toast the breadcrumbs in it, stirring constantly. Drain the cooked dumplings, turn them over in the breadcrumbs and sprinkle with sugar and cinnamon powder.

46.Cream of blood orange and carrot soup

ingredients

- 1 onion
- 2 cloves of garlic
- 4 carrots (large)
- 3-4 potatoes (small)
- 1000 ml of vegetable soup
- 1 tbsp sour cream
- 1 teaspoon ginger powder
- pepper
- salt
- 1 blood orange (squeezed)

preparation

1. For the blood orange and carrot cream soup, first coarsely chop the onion and garlic, peel and dice the carrots and potatoes.
2. Steam the onion and garlic in a little oil, stir in the ginger powder and deglaze with the juice of blood orange. Pour in the soup, add the carrot and potato pieces and simmer until they are done.
3. The blood orange carrot soup with a hand blender puree, season with sour cream, salt and pepper and serve.

47. Colorful potato mayonnaise salad

ingredients

- 1 cup (s) potatoes
- 1 cup (s) ham (diced)
- 1 cup (s) eggs (hard-boiled and chopped)
- 1 cup (s) of pickles
- 1 cup (s) of apples
- 1 cup (s) of onion
- 1 cup (s) of majo
- salt
- pepper

preparation

1. For the colorful potato and mayonnaise salad, cook potatoes until soft, peel and cut into cubes. Hard boil and chop eggs. Peel the

apple, remove the core and dice. Cut the pickle into small cubes. Peel onions and cut them into fine pieces. Cut the ham into cubes or strips.

2. Mix all ingredients, season with salt and pepper and stir in the mayonnaise. Let it steep in the refrigerator for at least 1 hour.

3. Serve the colorful potato and mayonnaise salad at room temperature!

48. Potato noodles

ingredients

- 750 g potatoes (floury)
- 130 g of flour
- 1 egg
- 1 pinch of salt
- oil
- nutmeg
- Rusks (crumbs)
- Sugar (brown)
- Apple compote

preparation

1. For the potato noodles, do not boil the potatoes too soft in the skin, peel them and pass them through the potato press or a

sieve; Mix with the eggs, flour, salt and a pinch of nutmeg to a batter. Shape these into finger-thick noodles and fry them in hot oil in a pan.

2. Turn in roasted, sweetened rusk crumbs and serve the potato noodles with apple compote.

49. Apple pie with potato topping

ingredients

Shortcrust:

- 240 g flour
- 160 g butter
- 80 g of icing sugar
- 1 egg
- 1 pinch of salt

Molding:

- 80 g butter
- 100 g of sugar
- 4 eggs
- 1 lemon (grated)
- 60 g almond kernels, shelled and ground
- 100 g potatoes (cooked, from the day before)

Also:

- 1000 g apples (Boskop)
- 30 g of sugar
- 1 lemon (juice)

preparation

1. Try this delicious cake recipe:
2. Shortcrust pastry: Knead together butter, sugar and egg and add the sifted flour and knead until a crumbly dough is formed. Then wrap in cling film and roughly
3. Rest in the refrigerator for 20 minutes. Grease a cake springform with a diameter of 26 cm and spread it out with the dough.
4. Remove the peel and core the apples and cut into 6-8 wedges according to size. Marinate with sugar and lemon juice.
5. Topping: Separate the eggs and beat half of the sugar with the butter, egg yolk and lemon zest. Stir in the ground almond kernels. Remove the cooked potatoes from the day before from the skin and grate or press through a press and also mix into the quantity. Finally, beat the egg white with the remaining sugar and fold into the potato mixture.

6. Pull the marinated apples through the glaze with a fork and place them evenly in the pan. Spread the rest of the icing evenly over the apples and then bake at 200 ° C top and bottom heat for about 45 minutes.

50. Potatoes with applesauce

ingredients

- 750 g potatoes
- 1 liter of water
- 125 g bacon (mixed)
- 3 onions
- Vinegar (to taste)
- 500 g applesauce (from the glass)
- 1 teaspoon sugar
- salt

preparation

1. For potatoes with applesauce, peel the potatoes. Bring to the boil in a saucepan with salted water and cook for 20 minutes. Drain and press into the pot while still hot through a press. Pour in the applesauce and stir the

mixture until thick and creamy, heat and add sugar.
2. Finely dice the peeled onions and bacon. Roast both in a frying pan until golden and add to the potatoes with applesauce. The potatoes with apple sauce to taste with vinegar and salt.

CONCLUSION

The potato diet is filling and draining. That brings a short-term minus on the scales, but in the long term the yo-yo effect threatens. Prolonged use of the mono diet is also not recommended as it can lead to nutrient deficiency.

Tip: Combine potatoes with quark or egg with vegetables, lettuce, herbs, vegetable fats, nuts and seeds. This is the healthier version of the potato diet and still lets the pounds drop off.

THE POTATO RECIPE COOKBOOK

50 EASY AND DELICIOUS POTATO RECIPES

KENNARD GRANT

INTRODUCTION

Potatoes contain significantly lower amounts of carbohydrates than other foods such as bread or pasta. It also produces greater satiety.

In principle, you should know that there are various myths about the potato. Among the most common is that it is a food that will make you gain kilos because it is composed mainly of sugars.

Potatoes contain complex carbohydrates, which are assimilated in a slower way, which produce a more gradual rise in blood sugar levels. It also helps to improve intestinal transit by providing fibers.

The potato or potato is a class of herbaceous plant that belongs to the Solanaceae family. There are innumerable myths about this tuber; among them, it does not provide any essential nutrient for the body.

Although many attribute the potato diet to helping them lose many pounds, no scientific study supports these claims.

Based on all this, we can say that the potato diet promises rapid weight loss by consuming potatoes basically, during the duration of the diet, which should not be longer than fourteen days. Although these claims have not yet been scientifically confirmed.

It is assumed that the loss of weight in this diet is due to the fact that the consumption of calories during the duration of this diet is very low . Among other things, because eating 0.9 to 2.3 grams of potatoes per day, although it seems like a lot, only equates to 530 to 1,300 calories, much less than the minimum intake that an adult should consume per day.

Possible advantages and disadvantages of this diet

There are many reasons to criticize the potato diet, but it has some potential benefits:

1. Potatoes are very nutritious. They are an excellent source of many essential vitamins and minerals, such as vitamin C, potassium, folate, and iron. It is not complicated. Although restrictive, the potato diet is fairly simple and easy to do . You simply have to consume potatoes for three, five or fourteen days.
2. It is accessible for any pocket. Potatoes are one of the cheapest foods available. It is high

in fiber, favoring the function of the intestine, being able to prevent obesity, heart disease and type 2 diabetes.

3. Despite these benefits, potatoes do not provide all the nutrients that are needed , the diet has to be varied to be healthy. Other possible disadvantages exist as the potato is the only ingredient in the diet.

1. Potatoes with curd cheese

- Cooking time 15 to 30 min
- Servings: 4

ingredients

- 1 kg of potatoes
- 500 g curd cheese
- 100 ml sour cream
- garlic
- butter
- salt
- 1 bunch of fresh herbs

preparation

1. For the potatoes with curd, first wash the potatoes well and cut them in half. Put water

in a saucepan, season with salt and cook the potatoes with their peel.

2. Stir the curd cheese with the sour cream and fresh herbs. Finely chop the garlic. Heat the butter in the pan and fry the garlic briefly. Mix the garlic into the mass.

3. Place the cooked potatoes on a plate (the potatoes stay in the skin) and serve with the curd cheese mixture.

2. Baked potatoes

- Cooking time 30 to 60 min
- Servings: 4

ingredients

- 500 g potatoes
- 125 g bacon (smoked)
- Frying fat
- 2 tbsp butter
- 1/2 cup (s) whipped cream
- 1/2 cup (s) of light beer
- 1 pc egg
- salt
- pepper
- Breadcrumbs
- Butter flakes
- onion rings

preparation

1. Peel the potatoes and cut into 0.5 cm thick slices; Cut the bacon into thin slices and fry in a little frying fat. Spread butter on an ovenproof dish and then add layers of potatoes and bacon; Whisk the whipped cream, beer, egg, salt and pepper and pour over the potatoes. Sprinkle with breadcrumbs, butter flakes and possibly onion rings and bake in the oven for about 30 minutes.

3. Szeged gulyas with potatoes

- Cooking time 30 to 60 min
- Servings: 4

ingredients

- 500 g sauerkraut
- 500 g pork (pork tenderloin)
- 2 onions (medium or 1 portion of roasted onions)
- salt
- pepper
- paprika
- 1 tbsp tomato paste
- garlic
- Caraway seed
- 1 cup of sour cream
- 500 g potatoes

preparation

1. Chop the onion and roast it with a little oil in a pan, cut the lung roast into cubes. Mix the sauerkraut with the diced meat and the roasted onion in a closed bowl and season with salt, pepper, paprika, tomato paste, crushed garlic and chopped caraway seeds.
2. Peel and quarter the potatoes. Cook in a perforated bowl.

4. Braised chicken with potatoes

- Cooking time More than 60 min
- Servings: 4

ingredients

- 1 chicken (organic, whole, approx. 1 kg)
- 1 bulb (s) of garlic
- 6 baby potatoes
- 10 sprig (s) of thyme
- 200 ml chicken soup
- 150 ml white wine
- 2 shallots
- 1 lemon (organic)
- 2 tbsp butter

preparation

1. For the braised chicken, preheat the oven to 160 ° C, cut the potatoes and garlic in half, and cut the lemon into slices.
2. Place the chicken breast up in an ovenproof dish (or in an ovenproof saucepan with a suitable lid), add the remaining ingredients as well as the wine and soup.
3. Season the chicken with salt and pepper, cover and braise for about 60 minutes, then remove the lid and fry for another 10-15 minutes.
4. Take the braised chicken out of the pot and serve with the potatoes and the gravy.

5. Black cumin potatoes with mint raita

- Cooking time 30 to 60 min
- Servings: 4

ingredients

- 500 g potatoes (waxy)
- 2 tbsp ghee
- 2 tbsp olive oil
- salt
- 2 tbsp black cumin
- 1 bunch of mint (fresh)
- 1 teaspoon fenugreek seeds
- 200 ml natural yogurt
- salt
- pepper

preparation

1. For the black cumin potatoes, cut the potatoes into slices. Melt the ghee in a small saucepan, mix with olive oil and salt.
2. Place the potatoes on a baking sheet and brush with the ghee-oil-salt mixture. Sprinkle with black cumin and bake in the oven at 200 degrees for about 30 minutes until golden brown.
3. Prick the thicker slices with a fork to see if they're already soft. While the potatoes are in the oven, finely chop the mint, grind the fenugreek seeds in a spice grinder (works faster) or in a mortar.
4. For the raita, stir the yoghurt, mint and fenugreek until smooth, season with salt and pepper. Serve the black cumin potatoes with the mint raita.

6. Potato in the beauty bath

- Cooking time 15 to 30 min
- Servings: 4

ingredients

- 1 kg potatoes (leftover from the day before)
- 200 g pickles (sweet and sour)
- 3 tbsp cream
- 60 g butter
- 40 grams of flour
- 3/4 l milk
- 2 teaspoons of soup powder
- salt
- pepper

preparation

1. For the potatoes in the beauty bath, melt the butter in a pan, add the flour by stirring constantly and over a low flame. Then stir in the milk with the whisk and simmer until it becomes nice and plump. Season with soup powder, salt and pepper, add the cream and season with the pickled gherkin water.
2. But be careful not to get too angry. Cut the cucumber and potatoes into bite-sized slices. Then simmer in the bechamel sauce for a few minutes and finally season with pepper.

7. Potato balm for the soul

- Cooking time 15 to 30 min
- Servings: 4

ingredients

- 2 avocado (very ripe)
- 4 tbsp Aceto Balsamico Bianco
- 3 tbsp aceto balsamic ice cream
- 2 clove (s) of garlic
- salt
- Mashed potatoes:
- 4 potatoes (large, floury)
- some milk
- 1 pc butter
- Salt
- olive oil

preparation

1. For the mashed potatoes, boil the potatoes in the skin until soft, peel and puree with a hand blender. Add warm milk, butter and salt. Peel the avocados, cut in half, cut lengthways into thin slices and fan out on plates.
2. Press the garlic and spread on the avocado. Marinate with vinegar and salt. Add a large dollop of mashed potatoes and drizzle with olive oil.

8. Baked potato eggs

- Cooking time 5 to 15 min
- Servings: 4

ingredients

- 2 baked potatoes (large)
- 40 g butter
- 4 eggs
- salt
- pepper
- Chives (for garnish)

preparation

1. For baked potato eggs, cook the potatoes in their skins until soft and cut in half. Hollow

out the halved potatoes a little with a coffee spoon, season with salt and pepper.

2. Add the butter and slide an egg into each half.

3. Place the filled potatoes in the oven preheated to 200 ° C for 10 minutes.

4. Remove the baked potato eggs, garnish with chives and serve.

9. potato pan

- Cooking time 30 to 60 min
- Servings: 4

ingredients

- 5 cloves of garlic (large)
- 1 sprig (s) of rosemary (large)
- 1.5kg of baby potatoes
- salt
- pepper
- 7 tbsp olive oil
- 250 g olives (black, with core)
- 1/8 l white wine (dry)

preparation

1. For the potato pan, peel and roughly chop the garlic, pluck the sprig of rosemary and peel the raw baby potatoes. Put the peeled

potatoes in an ovenproof dish so that they cover the bottom.
2. Then salt and pepper, sprinkle with garlic and rosemary, place the remaining branch on top and drizzle with the olive oil. Then place in the oven preheated to 200 ° C for 30 minutes.
3. Add olives and white wine and slide into the pipe for another 10 minutes.
4. Serve immediately.

10. Cremefine potato and pear gratin

- Cooking time More than 60 min
- Servings: 4

ingredients

For the Cremefine potato and pear gratin:

- 800 g potatoes
- 1 pear
- 250 ml Rama Cremefine for cooking
- Salt pepper

Delicious addition:

- 1 clove of garlic
- 80 g cheese (grated)

preparation

1. For the potato and pear gratin, peel the potatoes and cut into thin slices. Layer the

casserole dish in rows like a fan. Salt well and pepper to taste.

2. Preheat the oven to 200 ° C (gas: level 3, convection: 180 ° C). Quarter, core, peel and slice the pear. Place them well distributed between the potato slices.

3. Pour Cremefine on top and bake potato and pear gratin K in the preheated oven for about 50 minutes.

4. Goes very well with it: Crush the clove of garlic or cut it finely and mix with the Cremefine. Grated cheese, e.g. B. Emmentaler, sprinkle over the gratin and bake.

11. Baked potatoes with herring salad

- Cooking time More than 60 min
- Servings: 4

ingredients

For the potatoes:

- Vegetable oil (for brushing)
- 4 potatoes (large, mostly waxy, approx. 250 g each)
- salt
- Pepper (from the mill)

For the herring salad:

- 6 double matjes fillets

- 1 onion (large, mild)
- 2 apples (red)
- 120 g sour cream
- 80 g yogurt
- 60 g mayonnaise
- 1-2 tbsp apple cider vinegar
- 1 squirt of lemon juice
- salt
- 1 pinch of sugar
- Pepper (from the mill)
- Dill (freshly chopped, for garnish)

preparation

1. For baked potatoes with herring salad, first preheat the oven to 200 ° C top and bottom heat. Brush 4 pieces of aluminum foil with oil.
2. Pierce the potatoes several times with a fork, season with salt, pepper and wrap each time tightly in aluminum foil. Place the baked potatoes on a baking sheet and cook in the oven for about 1 hour until soft.
3. Pat the herring fillets dry and cut into bite-sized pieces. Peel the onion, cut into eighths and cut into fine strips. Wash and quarter the apples and remove the core. Halve the quarters lengthways and cut across into pieces.

4. Mix the sour cream with the yogurt, mayonnaise, vinegar and lemon juice until smooth. Season the dressing with salt, sugar and pepper. Mix in all the prepared salad ingredients and season the herring salad to taste.
5. Remove the potatoes, wrap them out of the foil, cut them crosswise, push them apart a little and let them evaporate briefly. Pour in the herring salad, grind lightly with pepper and serve baked potatoes with herring salad sprinkled with dill.

12. Matjes fillets with new potatoes and brunch

- Cooking time 30 to 60 min
- Servings: 4

ingredients

- 800 g potatoes
- salt
- 1 pc egg
- 1 bunch of radishes
- 1 bunch of chives
- 200 g Brunch Classic
- 50 ml of milk
- 2 tbsp lemon juice
- Pepper (freshly ground)
- 8 matjes fillet

preparation

1. Wash the potatoes and cook in salted water for about 25 minutes. Boil the egg hard for about 10 minutes. Wash and clean the radishes and cut into fine sticks. Wash the chives, pat dry and cut into rolls.
2. Peel the egg, dice it finely and mix it with the brunch, radishes, chives, milk and lemon juice. Serve with herring fillets and potatoes.

13. Herbal fish with potato zucchini vegetables

- Cooking time 30 to 60 min

ingredients

Potato and zucchini vegetables:

- 400 g small, greasy potatoes
- 1 piece of zucchini (approx. 200 g)
- Salt pepper
- 2 sprigs of thyme
- 2 Tea spoons olive oil
- Aluminum foil

Herb fish:

- 2 pieces. fillets of a lean fish (cod, saithe)
- 2 tbsp lemon juice
- Salt pepper

- 1 teaspoon grated lemon peel (untreated)
- Herbs (at will)
- Aluminum foil

preparation

1. Preheat the oven to 180 ° C.
2. For the potato and zucchini vegetables, wash and brush the potatoes. Pre-cook in a steamer for about 15 minutes, peel and cut into large pieces. Cut the zucchini into thin slices.
3. Place two pieces of aluminum foil on top, distribute the sliced potatoes and zucchini in the middle, season with salt and pepper, put a sprig of thyme on each and drizzle with olive oil. Seal the aluminum pack tightly.
4. For the herb fish, place a fish fillet seasoned with lemon juice, salt and pepper on two more pieces of aluminum foil, sprinkle with lemon zest and herbs. Seal the package tightly.
5. Place all four aluminum packets on a baking sheet and cook in the preheated oven for about 20 minutes.
6. Then open, serve the herb fish with the potato and zucchini vegetables.

14. Salmon fillet with asparagus and vegetables

- Cooking time More than 60 min
- Servings: 4

ingredients

- 500 g asparagus (white)
- 2 zucchini (small)
- 1 pc leek (small)
- 600 g salmon slices
- 500 g potatoes

preparation

1. Peel the potatoes, cut the vegetables into not too small pieces, salt the salmon and drizzle with lemon juice.
2. Put the potatoes in a perforated bowl. Layer the vegetables separately in a perforated

bowl and also put the salmon fillets in their own lightly greased perforated bowl.

3. First put the potatoes in the steamer. Cooking setting for vegetables at 100 ° C for 30 minutes.

4. After 20 minutes, put the asparagus and leek in the steamer, then add the salmon and zucchini for the last 5 minutes.

15. Spring salmon from the steamer

- Cooking time 15 to 30 min
- Servings: 4

ingredients

- 1 bunch of spring onions
- 500 g fish fillets (Iglo TK salmon)
- salt
- pepper
- Dill
- 1 lemon
- 250 ml whipped cream
- 3 eggs
- 2 potatoes (small)
- Cherry tomatoes

preparation

1. Chop the spring onions and fry them a little. Spread in a large unperforated bowl.
2. Cut the salmon into approx. 1 cm cubes and spread over them.
3. Beat the whipped cream with the eggs, grate in the potatoes, season and spread over the salmon.
4. Cook in the steamer at 100 degrees for about 20 minutes.
5. Serve with halved cherry tomatoes and dill sauce (dill, salt, sour cream).

16. Salmon in a bed of vegetables

- Cooking time 30 to 60 min
- Servings: 4

ingredients

- 400 g carrots
- 200 g zucchini
- 4 pcs. spring onions
- 600 g potatoes
- salt
- pepper
- 600 g salmon fillet (preferably wild salmon)
- some lemon juice
- Lemon wedges (for the garnish)

preparation

1. For salmon in a bed of vegetables, peel the potatoes, wash the carrots and zucchini and

cut into pieces that are not too small. Peel the spring onions and cut into strips. Put the potatoes in a perforated bowl.

2. Place the vegetables in another perforated cooking container and season with salt and pepper. Season the fish fillet, drizzle with lemon juice and also place in its own, lightly greased perforated bowl.

3. First steam the potatoes for 30 minutes. After 18 minutes, put the salmon in the steamer, reduce the temperature to 85 ° C. Steam the vegetables for the last 6 minutes.

4. Salt the potatoes to taste. Arrange the potatoes and vegetables on plates, place salmon slices on top of the vegetables. Serve topped with the lemon wedge.

17. Herring salad with pomegranate

- Cooking time More than 60 min
- Servings: 4

ingredients

- 8 pieces of herring fillets
- 1 apple (e.g .: Boskop)
- 200 g potatoes (cooked)
- 3 tbsp vinegar
- 1 teaspoon sugar
- 4 tbsp mayonnaise
- 250 g sour cream
- pepper
- salt
- 1 onion (small, chopped)
- 1 pomegranate

preparation

1. For the herring salad with pomegranate, debone and dry herring fillets. Cut the fillets into small cubes.
2. Peel and dice the apple and the boiled potatoes.
3. Roll the pomegranate on a firm surface with a little pressure, then cut it open and remove the pomegranate seeds.
4. Whisk the mayonnaise with the sour cream, vinegar, sugar, pepper and salt. Peel and finely chop the onion and stir into the sauce.
5. Fold the herrings, apple pieces, potatoes and pomegranate apple seeds into the sour cream mixture.
6. Let the herring salad with pomegranate steep for about 1 hour and then serve.

18. Char with wild garlic coconut puree

- Cooking time 30 to 60 min

ingredients

- 4 pieces of char
- 400 g floury potatoes
- 5 g wild garlic
- 150 ml coconut milk
- 3 tbsp oil
- 1 tbsp sesame oil for frying
- nutmeg
- salt

preparation

1. Boil the potatoes in salted water until soft, peel them while still warm, press them through the potato press and place in a bowl. Wash the wild garlic, puree with 3

tablespoons of oil and mix into the potatoes together with the coconut milk and mix everything well with the whisk. Season to taste with salt and nutmeg. Heat a non-stick pan, pour in the sesame oil and fry the fish fillets seasoned with salt and pepper on both sides for about 2 minutes. Arrange the puree on plates, the fish fillets next to or on top.

19.Gröstl from the smoked catfish

- Cooking time 30 to 60 min
- Servings: 2

ingredients

- 300 g of cauliflower (cauliflower)
- 20 g liquid nut butter
- 10 g yogurt
- 20 ml aged balsamic vinegar
- Sea salt, pepper from the mill
- 3 potatoes
- 1 tbsp peanut oil
- 240 g river catfish, smoked
- salt

preparation

1. Cook half of the cauliflower until soft and puree with the nut butter, yogurt and balsamic vinegar, season and keep warm.
2. Divide the rest of the cauliflower into florets and cook until al dente. Cut the potatoes into cubes and cook. Fry cauliflower florets and potato cubes in peanut oil.
3. Cut the catfish fillet into cubes, place on a plate, season with salt, wrap with heat-resistant foil and let it simmer at approx. 90 ° C for 10 minutes. Serve with cauliflower puree and Gröstl and drizzle with balsamic nut butter emulsion.

20. Carp in black beer batter with green potato salad

- Cooking time 15 to 30 min

ingredients

- 4 pieces of carp fillets
- salt
- cumin
- Lemon juice
- 1/4 l black beer
- 2 pieces of egg yolks
- 250 g of flour

For the potato salad:

- Potatoes
- Wild garlic pesto (or basil pesto)
- arugula
- sour cream
- vinegar
- oil
- salt

preparation

1. For the potato salad, boil and peel the potatoes, cut into small pieces. Mix the pesto, cream, vinegar, oil and salt to a creamy marinade.

2. Cut the carp fillet into strips and season with salt, pepper, cumin and lemon juice.
3. Mix the egg yolk, flour and black beer into a batter, pull the fish fillets through the batter and fry in hot fat.
4. Arrange the rocket on plates, place the green potato salad on top and place the carp fillets on top and serve.

21.Minced meat with mashed potatoes

- Cooking time More than 60 min
- Servings: 2

ingredients

- 6 tomatoes
- 6 shallots
- 1 clove of garlic
- Oil (for frying)
- 500 g minced meat
- salt
- Pepper (from the mill)

For the mashed potatoes:

- 800 g potatoes
- 350 ml milk
- 80 g butter (in flakes)

- salt
- Pepper (white)
- 1 pinch of nutmeg (ground)

preparation

1. For minced meat with mashed potatoes, first peel the potatoes, chop them roughly and cook them in salted water until they are soft. Pour off and squeeze out. Heat the milk and mix with the potatoes. Stir in butter. Season with salt, pepper and nutmeg.
2. Blanch the tomatoes and peel off the skin. Dice the pulp. Peel and finely dice the shallots. Peel and press or finely chop the garlic.
3. Heat the oil and fry the shallots and garlic in it. Add the minced meat and fry well. Add the tomatoes. Let simmer for about half an hour. Season to taste with salt and pepper. Puree if necessary.
4. Serve minced meat with mashed potatoes.

22. Meat dumplings

ingredients

For the dough:

- 500 g potatoes
- 10 g butter
- 30 g wheat semolina
- 120 g flour (handy)
- 1 pc egg
- salt
- nutmeg

For the fullness:

- 1 tbsp sunflower oil
- 100 g onions
- 200 g minced meat (mixed)
- 1 tbsp QimiQ
- salt

- Mustard, pepper
- Marjoram, garlic

preparation

1. Prepare the potato dough: peel, quarter and steam the potatoes. Press the potatoes on a floured pastry board, spread the flakes of butter on top and briefly knead together with the remaining ingredients to form a dough.
2. Prepare the filling: finely chop the onions, roast them in oil, add the minced meat, roast briefly, thicken with QimiQ and season.
3. Deliver water.
4. Shape the dough into a roll, cut into slices, spread the filling on top, form dumplings and close tightly.
5. Let the dumplings soak in salted water for about 10-15 minutes.
6. Take out the meat dumplings with a sieve scoop and serve.

23. Spinach with boiled beef and roasted potatoes

ingredients

- 1 packet of frozen spinach
- 1 clove (s) garlic (pressed through)
- 6 potatoes (about 300 g, cooked and chopped up)
- 1 onion (chopped into small pieces)
- some oil (for frying)
- salt
- 300 g beef (cooked, e.g. shoulder pecker, lean chisel)
- Pepper (freshly ground)

preparation

1. Thaw the spinach and heat it in a saucepan.

165

2. Peel and squeeze the garlic clove and stir into the spinach, mix well.
3. Sauté the onion in oil, add the potatoes, season with salt and pepper and fry until crispy, turning frequently.
4. Cut the beef into slices.
5. Put the spinach on the plate, place the beef on top, add the potatoes and serve immediately.

24. Roast onion with mashed potatoes

- Cooking time 30 to 60 min

ingredients

- 500 g potatoes (floury)
- 100 ml milk
- 1 onion
- 2 slice (s) of Beiried (200 g each)
- 150 ml veal stock
- 150 ml red wine
- salt
- pepper
- nutmeg
- paprika
- Flour
- butter
- oil

preparation

1. Peel the potatoes, quarter them and boil them in salted water, then drain them and press them through the press while they are still hot. Stir in hot milk, 1 tbsp butter, salt and nutmeg with a whisk and keep the puree warm.
2. Cut the onion into thin slices, season with salt, pepper and paprika and dust with flour, fry in hot oil until golden brown.
3. Season the meat with salt and pepper and sear it on both sides in a pan in oil, then let it simmer for a few minutes over low heat.
4. Take the meat out of the pan and keep it warm. Deglaze the roast set with the stock and red wine and reduce by half.
5. Serve the meat with the mashed potatoes and the onions, pour the sauce over them and serve.

25. Liver and potato dumplings with lettuce

ingredients

- 350 g veal liver
- 350 g potatoes (cooked)
- 2 eggs
- 100 g of flour
- 2 tbsp lard (or oil)
- 120 g breadcrumbs
- 120 g onions (finely chopped)
- 2 cloves of garlic (finely chopped)
- 1/2 tbsp marjoram (chopped)
- salt
- pepper
- 200 g lamb's lettuce
- Vinegar (and oil for marinating)
- Oil (for frying)

preparation

1. Roughly mince the veal liver or chop it very finely. Press the cooked potatoes through a potato press. Sauté the chopped onions and garlic in hot fat, mix with the liver, the pressed potatoes and the eggs. Season with salt, pepper and marjoram.
2. Mix the flour and breadcrumbs into the mixture. Pour oil into a pan finger high and heat. Use a spoon to cut out cams from the mass and bake them out. Lift out and drain. Marinate the lamb's lettuce with vinegar, oil and salt and serve with the dumplings.

26. Root vegetable soup with potatoes

- Cooking time 15 to 30 min

ingredients

- 250 g carrots (yellow)
- 250 g carrots
- 200 g parsnips
- 5 potatoes (small)
- Parsley (fresh)
- 1 tbsp rapeseed oil
- pepper
- Vegetable soup cubes

preparation

1. For the root vegetable soup with potatoes, peel the carrots, yellow carrots and parsnips, cut into slices or dice. Roast in rapeseed oil, pour water, and let boil.
2. A quarter of an hour later add the potatoes and cook everything together until soft. Season to taste with pepper and vegetable soup seasoning. At the end add the washed and chopped parsley.
3. The root vegetable soup with potato serve.

27. Potato and mushroom soup

ingredients

- 4 potatoes (approx. 500g)
- 3 carrots (approx. 300g)
- 150 g celeriac
- 2 pcs. Onions
- 150 g mushrooms
- 250 ml whipped cream
- 1 l vegetable soup
- 2 tbsp flour
- 1 tbsp soy sauce
- marjoram
- Lovage
- Savory
- Caraway seed
- nutmeg
- Fechel seeds
- pepper

- salt
- 1 bunch of chives
- 1/2 bunch of parsley
- 6 teaspoons of horseradish cream (add 1 teaspoon per serving)

preparation

1. For the potato and mushroom soup, dice the onions very small and fry until golden. Dice the mushrooms and add to the onions.
2. Dice the potatoes, carrots and celeriac, add and sauté briefly. Add flour and fry briefly. Pour the soup on top, season with marjoram, lovage, savory, caraway seeds, nutmeg, fennel seeds, salt and pepper.
3. Bring to the boil briefly, add the whipped cream, then let steep on the lowest level until the vegetables are cooked through.
4. Add the chives and parsley, season well and serve the potato and mushroom soup with the horseradish.

28. Potato soup

- Cooking time 15 to 30 min

ingredients

- 450 g potatoes
- 1 leek (s)
- 200 g carrots
- 2 pcs. Onions
- approx. 150 g celeriac
- l soup
- Bay leaves
- marjoram
- chives
- salt
- 1 tbsp flour
- Savory
- Lovage
- parsley

- pepper

preparation

1. For the potato soup, dice the onion, roughly chop the vegetables, fry the onions in a saucepan until golden, add the leek and flour and fry briefly.
2. Add the remaining vegetables and bay leaves and pour on the soup. Let simmer until the potatoes are done.
3. Now add the marjoram, savory and lovage and let it steep. Before serving, add the chives and parsley to the potato soup.

29. Potato soup with chanterelles

ingredients

- 1 pc onion
- Olive oil (for braising)
- 300 g potatoes
- 400 ml of vegetable soup
- 250 ml soy cuisine
- 2 pieces of bay leaves
- 1 teaspoon marjoram
- 1 teaspoon ginger (grated)
- 150 g chanterelles
- salt
- Parsley (chopped, for sprinkling)
- pepper

preparation

1. For the potato soup, cut the onion into small pieces. Peel and dice the potatoes, clean the chanterelles and cut them smaller if necessary.
2. Sauté the onion in the olive oil until translucent. Roast the potato cubes briefly, pour in the soup and soy cuisine, add the spices and simmer for 10 minutes until the potatoes are soft.
3. In the meantime, briefly toast the chanterelles in olive oil and add to the soup 3 minutes before the end of the boil. Sprinkle the soup with parsley before serving.

30. Cabbage potato soup

ingredients

- 500 g potatoes
- 3 onions
- 750 g white cabbage (sliced)
- 1 liter of soup
- 500 g bacon (lean)
- 3 tbsp caraway seeds
- 1 tbsp flour
- 1 tbsp butter
- 3 tbsp sour cream
- 1 tbsp salt
- pepper

preparation

3. For the cabbage potato soup, sauté grated white cabbage, peeled potatoes and lean bacon cut into cubes in the soup until soft. Season to taste with salt, caraway seeds and pepper.
4. Before serving, sauté the finely chopped onions in a little butter, dust with flour, stir with a little sour cream and stir into the cabbage-potato soup .

31. Potato soup with sausages

ingredients

- 1 pack of Tk soup green
- 800 g potatoes
- 1 onion
- 30 g butter
- 750 ml beef soup ((instant))
- 125 ml whipped cream
- salt
- pepper
- Paprika (noble sweet)
- 4 frankfurters
- 1 bunch of parsley

preparation

4. Defrost the soup greens. Peel and rinse potatoes, cut into cubes. Peel and chop the

onion, sauté in butter until translucent. Add potatoes and fry briefly. Pour in clear soup, cook everything together for 12-15 minutes.

5. Remove 1/3 of the potatoes, grind the rest in the saucepan. Put the remaining potato pieces with the thawed soup greens and whipped cream in the saucepan again. Soup 6-8 min.

6. Season with peppers, salt and pepper. Sauté Frankfurt sausages in hot water, remove and drain. Cut into small slices. In the potato soup form. Rinse the parsley, shake dry, chop finely and sprinkle over it before serving.

32. pumpkin cream soup

ingredients

- 1 pumpkin (Hokaido)
- 2 onions
- 2 cloves of garlic
- 5 potatoes
- 1 l vegetable soup
- 250 ml sour cream (or 200 ml whipped cream)
- Pumpkin seed oil
- salt

preparation

5. For the pumpkin cream soup, finely chop the onion and garlic. Cut the pumpkin and potato into small pieces.
6. Heat oil in a large saucepan and lightly sweat the onion pieces and garlic. Pour on the soup and bring to the boil. Add the pumpkin and potato pieces and simmer for 20 minutes.
7. Puree the soup after the 20 minutes. Stir in the sour cream or whipped cream well and season with salt.
8. Arrange in a soup plate and decorate the pumpkin cream soup with the pumpkin seed oil.

33. Potato soup with tofu skewers

ingredients

- 750 g potatoes
- 3 pcs. Onions
- 2 tbsp olive oil
- 1 l vegetable soup
- 2 zucchini (small)
- 200 g tofu
- 1 tbsp sesame seeds
- salt
- 250 ml soy (cooking cream)
- 1 tbsp mustard
- marjoram
- pepper

preparation

6. For the potato soup with tofu skewers, peel and chop the potatoes and onions. Heat 1 tbsp oil in a saucepan and sauté the onion briefly.
7. Add the potatoes, deglaze with the soup. Bring to the boil and cook for 15 minutes. Cut the zucchini and tofu into slices and stick them alternately on wooden skewers.
8. Fry the skewers in the hot oil until golden brown while turning. Sprinkle with sesame seeds and season with salt and pepper.
9. Puree the soup, mix the cooking cream and mustard and add to the soup, bring to the boil again. Season with salt and pepper.
10. The potato soup with tofu skewers serve.

34. Alkaline potato soup

ingredients

- 500 ml of water
- 1 vegetable soup cube
- 1 pinch of acerola powder
- 8 potatoes (medium)
- 100 g carrots (finely grated)
- 1 leek (leek, stick)
- 1 kg onion (finely chopped)
- 2 tbsp cream
- 1 tbsp dille (fresh, finely chopped)
- 1 tbsp butter
- sea-salt
- 1 pinch of pepper
- 1 pinch of paprika powder

preparation

6. For the alkaline potato soup, sauté the onion in butter until translucent. Pour water on.
7. Add potatoes and finely chopped vegetables and bring everything to a boil.
8. Simmer on a low level for 15 minutes and then puree. Refine with cream and season with the spices.
9. Sprinkle the finely chopped dill on top.
10. The acerola powder just before Servierenin the Basic Potato Soup add.

35. Broad bean stew

ingredients

- 3 kg broad beans (fresh)
- 400 g of lamb
- 750 g potatoes
- 40 g butter
- 400 ml of water
- Savory
- Pepper (ground)
- salt

preparation

1. For the broad bean stew, chop the meat into small cubes.

2. Peel, wash and dice the potatoes. Heat the butter, turn the meat and turn it lightly brown in it, season with salt and pepper.
3. Add the savory, potatoes, beans and water, let simmer for approx. 1 1/2 hours. Season the broad bean stew with salt and pepper and serve hot.

36. Sweet potato rolls

ingredients

- 250 g potatoes (floury)
- 250 g wheat flour (smooth)
- 250 g whole wheat flour
- 1 package dry yeast
- 80 g of sugar
- 1 pc egg
- 80 g yogurt (low fat)
- 1/8 l skimmed milk (lukewarm, or water)

preparation

1. Steam the potatoes in their skins for about 20 minutes. Peel while hot and press through a potato press. Let cool down slightly.

2. Mix in the flour, yeast, sugar, egg and yoghurt. Pour in liquid. At the beginning only about 100ml and the rest only when needed. Knead the dough vigorously with the food processor for about 5 minutes.
3. If necessary, add a little more liquid so that the dough has a smooth consistency. Cover and let the dough rise in a warm place for approx. 45 - 30 minutes.
4. Then form 15 rolls and place on a perforated, greased (or lined with parchment paper) cooking insert.
5. Let rise for another 10 minutes. Steam for 45 minutes.

37. Potato spirals on a skewer

ingredients

- 4 potatoes (large)
- 2 tbsp oil
- 1 pinch of thyme (dried, rubbed)
- salt
- Pepper (from the mill)
- 4 wooden skewers

preparation

1. For the potato spirals on the skewer, first preheat the oven to 190 ° C hot air. Line a baking sheet with parchment paper. Peel the potatoes and put them in cold water if necessary.

2. Stick the potato lengthways on a wooden skewer. Cut all around with a sharp knife up to the skewer and turn the skewer so that spirals arise. Pull apart a little. Place on the baking sheet.
3. Mix the oil with salt, pepper and dried thyme and brush the potato spirals with it. The potato spirals on a spit for about 20 minutes to bake.

38. Potato spread

ingredients

- 2 potatoes (e.g. Ditta)
- 1/2 onion
- 1/2 clove of garlic
- 2 tbsp low-fat yogurt
- 1 tbsp sour cream (sour cream)
- Chives (and / or parsley)
- salt
- Pepper (from the mill)

preparation

1. Boil the potatoes and let them cool.
2. Then peel and press through the potato press or mash very finely.

3. Peel and finely chop the onion, crush the garlic, cut the chives into rolls.
4. Mix the potatoes, onions, garlic with yoghurt, sour cream and chives, season with salt and pepper.

39. Skordalia (potato and garlic paste)

ingredients

- 400 g potatoes (semi-hard boiling)
- 4-6 cloves of garlic (very finely chopped)
- 125 ml chicken soup
- 50 g olives (black)
- 5 tbsp olive oil
- 1 lemon
- Sea salt (from the mill)
- Pepper (from the mill)

preparation

1. Boil the peeled potatoes until soft, allow to cool and roughly mash them with a fork in a bowl. Stir in the garlic and chicken soup and

gradually stir in the olive oil until a creamy mixture is formed. Season with lemon juice, salt and pepper. Core, chop the olives and then stir in. Serve lukewarm or cold.

40. Alkaline wild garlic wedges

ingredients

- 20 g wild garlic
- 100 g yogurt (0.1% fat)
- 400 g potatoes (raw)
- 25 g rapeseed oil
- 1 g pepper
- 25 ml of water
- 1 g salt

preparation

1. For basic wild garlic wedges, first wash the potatoes and cut into wedges . Finely puree the wild garlic with water and oil. Season the wild garlic oil with salt. Marinate the potatoes with oil and bake them in the oven at 180 ° C

for about 30-35 minutes (the cooking time depends on the size of the cracks).

2. In the meantime, mix yoghurt with sour cream and season with salt and pepper. Serve alkaline wild garlic wedges with yogurt sauce.

41. Herring salad with celery

ingredients

- 8 pieces of herring fillets
- 1 apple
- 200 g potatoes (cooked)
- 3 tbsp vinegar
- 1 teaspoon sugar
- 4 tbsp mayonnaise
- 250 g sour cream
- pepper
- salt
- 2 stick (s) celery

preparation

1. Debone and dry the herring fillets. Cut the fillets into small cubes.
2. Peel and dice the apple and the boiled potatoes.

3. Cut the celery into small pieces.
4. Whisk the mayonnaise with the sour cream, vinegar, sugar, pepper and salt.
5. Fold the herrings, apple pieces, potatoes and celery into the sour cream mixture.
6. Let it steep for about 1 hour and then serve.

42. Light onion spread with apple and bacon

ingredients

- 200 g potatoes
- 80 g hamburger bacon
- 1/2 onion
- 1/2 apple (sour)
- 2 tbsp sour cream
- 1 teaspoon orange juice
- salt
- pepper

preparation

1. For the light onion spread with apple and bacon, peel and dice the potatoes and cook them in salted water until soft. Cut the bacon

into small cubes and fry in a pan until crispy, drain on kitchen paper.

2. Cut the onion into small cubes and briefly boil over in a little salted water, rinse in a colander and drain well.

3. Chop the apple into small cubes, press the potatoes through the potato press or mash them with a fork, mix well with the sour cream. Add the remaining ingredients (leave a few diced bacon for garnish) and stir well.

4. Finally, season the light onion spread .

43. Herring salad with pear and nuts

ingredients

- 8 pieces of herring fillets
- 200 g potatoes (cooked)
- 2 pear
- 250 g sour cream
- pepper
- salt
- 1 onion (small, chopped)
- 1 teaspoon sugar
- 3 tbsp vinegar
- 4 tbsp mayonnaise
- 30 g walnuts (roughly chopped)

preparation

1. Debone and dry the herring fillets. Cut the fillets into small cubes.
2. Peel and dice the pears and the boiled potatoes.
3. Whisk the mayonnaise with the sour cream, vinegar, sugar, pepper and salt. Peel and finely chop the onion and stir into the sauce.
4. Fold the herrings, pear pieces, walnuts and potatoes into the sour cream mixture.
5. Let it steep for about 1 hour and then serve.

44. Herring salad with melon

ingredients

- 8 pieces of herring fillets
- 200 g potatoes (cooked)
- 1/2 piece of sugar melon
- 1 onion (small, chopped)
- 1 teaspoon sugar
- 3 tbsp vinegar
- 250 g sour cream
- 4 tbsp mayonnaise
- pepper
- salt

preparation

1. Debone and dry the herring fillets. Cut the fillets into small cubes.
2. Peel the melon and cut into small pieces. Peel and dice the boiled potatoes.
3. Whisk the mayonnaise with the sour cream, vinegar, sugar, pepper and salt. Peel and finely chop the onion and stir into the sauce.
4. Fold the herrings, pieces of melon and potatoes into the sour cream mixture.
5. Let it steep for about 1 hour and then serve.

45. Potato buns

ingredients

- 600 g potatoes
- 200 grams of flour
- 1 egg
- salt
- 1 pinch of nutmeg
- Flour (for rolling)
- Clarified butter (for baking)
- Butter (liquid to drizzle over)
- 3 tbsp sour cream
- Buttermilk (as desired, sour milk or yogurt, as well as cold)

preparation

1. First, boil, strain and peel the potatoes.

2. Press through a sieve and knead with the flour, egg, salt and nutmeg to form a loose dough.
3. First form rolls as thick as a thumb from the finished dough and cut off rolls approx. 2 to 3 cm long with a dampened knife.
4. Flour well and brown all around in hot clarified butter until golden yellow (a process that is best done layer by layer, because not all paunzen can fit in one pan).
5. Drizzle the finished Paunzen with melted butter and serve with buttermilk, sour milk or yoghurt and cold sauerkraut as desired.

46. Potato Vegetable Strudel

ingredients

- 250 g potatoes (floury)
- 50 g carrots
- 200 g broccoli
- salt
- pepper
- 100 g cream cheese (low in fat)
- Fresh herbs
- 1 piece of strudel sheet
- Milk for brushing

preparation

1. For the potato and vegetable strudel, boil the potatoes, let them cool down, peel and mash them. Clean the carrots and cut into cubes.
2. Wash broccoli and cut into florets. Steam the carrots and broccoli in a little water until they are al dente. Mix the mashed potatoes with the cream cheese, season and add the chopped herbs.
3. Place the strudel sheet on a baking tray lined with baking paper and spread the potato and cream cheese mixture on top. Roll up the Studel and brush with milk.
4. Bake in the preheated oven at 170 ° C for 30 minutes.

47. Herring salad with orange

ingredients

- 8 pieces of herring fillets
- 200 g potatoes (cooked)
- 2 pieces of orange
- salt
- 1 onion (small, chopped)
- 1 teaspoon sugar
- 3 tbsp vinegar
- 250 g sour cream
- 4 tbsp mayonnaise
- pepper

preparation

6. Debone and dry the herring fillets. Cut the fillets into small cubes.
7. Peel the oranges, remove the white skin and cut out fine pieces of fillet. Peel and dice the boiled potatoes.
8. Whisk the mayonnaise with the sour cream, vinegar, sugar, pepper and salt. Peel and finely chop the onion and stir into the sauce.
9. Fold the herrings, orange pieces and potatoes into the sour cream mixture.
10. Let it steep for about 1 hour and then serve.

48. Herring salad with grapes

ingredients

- 8 pieces of herring fillets
- 200 g potatoes (cooked)
- 300 g of grapes
- 3 tbsp vinegar
- 250 g sour cream
- 4 tbsp mayonnaise
- pepper
- salt
- 1 onion (small, chopped)
- sugar

preparation

6. Debone and dry the herring fillets. Cut the fillets into small cubes.
7. Halve the individual grapes. Peel and dice the boiled potatoes.
8. Whisk the mayonnaise with the sour cream, vinegar, sugar, pepper and salt. Peel and finely chop the onion and stir into the sauce.
9. Fold the herrings, pieces of grapes and potatoes into the sour cream mixture.
10. Let it steep for about 1 hour and then serve.

49. Herring salad with avocado

ingredients

- 8 pieces of herring fillets
- 200 g potatoes (cooked)
- 1 apple
- 4 tbsp mayonnaise
- 250 g sour cream
- pepper
- salt
- 1 onion (small, chopped)
- 1 teaspoon sugar
- 3 tbsp vinegar
- 2 pieces avocado

preparation

7. Debone and dry the herring fillets. Cut the fillets into small cubes.

8. Peel and dice the apple and the boiled potatoes.
9. Peel the avocado and cut the pulp into small pieces.
10. Whisk the mayonnaise with the sour cream, vinegar, sugar, pepper and salt. Peel and finely chop the onion and stir into the sauce.
11. Fold the herrings, apple pieces, avocado pieces and potatoes into the sour cream mixture.
12. Let it steep for about 1 hour and then serve.

50. fried potatoes

ingredients

- 500 g potatoes
- salt
- pepper
- Caraway seed

preparation

1. For the fried potatoes, preheat the oven to 180 ° C.
2. Wash the potatoes thoroughly, do not peel, cut into 1 cm thick slices.
3. Place on a baking sheet lined with baking paper, season with salt, pepper and, if necessary, sprinkle with caraway seeds.

4. Fry the fried potatoes in the oven for about 20 minutes.

51. Braised chicken with potatoes

- Cooking time More than 60 min
- Servings: 4

ingredients

- 1 chicken (organic, whole, approx. 1 kg)
- 1 bulb (s) of garlic
- 6 baby potatoes
- 10 sprig (s) of thyme
- 200 ml chicken soup
- 150 ml white wine
- 2 shallots
- 1 lemon (organic)
- 2 tbsp butter

preparation

5. For the braised chicken, preheat the oven to 160 ° C, cut the potatoes and garlic in half, and cut the lemon into slices.
6. Place the chicken breast up in an ovenproof dish (or in an ovenproof saucepan with a suitable lid), add the remaining ingredients as well as the wine and soup.
7. Season the chicken with salt and pepper, cover and braise for about 60 minutes, then remove the lid and fry for another 10-15 minutes.
8. Take the braised chicken out of the pot and serve with the potatoes and the gravy.

52. Liver and potato dumplings with lettuce

ingredients

- 350 g veal liver
- 350 g potatoes (cooked)
- 2 eggs
- 100 g of flour
- 2 tbsp lard (or oil)
- 120 g breadcrumbs
- 120 g onions (finely chopped)
- 2 cloves of garlic (finely chopped)
- 1/2 tbsp marjoram (chopped)
- salt
- pepper
- 200 g lamb's lettuce
- Vinegar (and oil for marinating)
- Oil (for frying)

preparation

3. Roughly mince the veal liver or chop it very finely. Press the cooked potatoes through a potato press. Sauté the chopped onions and garlic in hot fat, mix with the liver, the pressed potatoes and the eggs. Season with salt, pepper and marjoram.
4. Mix the flour and breadcrumbs into the mixture. Pour oil into a pan finger high and heat. Use a spoon to cut out cams from the mass and bake them out. Lift out and drain. Marinate the lamb's lettuce with vinegar, oil and salt and serve with the dumplings.

CONCLUSION

Potatoes contain fewer carbohydrates, take up more, and have fewer calories than rice or pasta. Therefore, it is the perfect accompaniment if you want to reduce the calories consumed.

Its starch turns into resistant starch after cooling, which cannot be divided by the body.

If the plants, always try not to get the sun before harvesting them. Otherwise, they will produce solanine, a natural poison. If a potato turns green, this means that its solanine content is high and you should avoid eating them.

New potatoes are the most suitable for cooking. Even those with somewhat brittle skin offer the same nutritional values and are just as healthy. Sweet potatoes or sweet potatoes contain more natural sugars than the classic version.

Lightning Source UK Ltd.
Milton Keynes UK
UKHW021110150822
407314UK00006B/105